90 Blessings in 90 Days:

How to Live in the Soul

Ellen Grace O'Brian

CSE Press
San Jose, California

CSE Press
1146 University Avenue
San Jose, California 95126
(408) 283-0221
e-mail: info@csecenter.org
web site: www.csecenter.org

CSE Press is the publishing department
of Center for Spiritual Enlightenment

My teacher told me one thing:
Live in the soul.

–Lad Ded

To my teacher, Roy Eugene Davis, with gratitude

Other Books by Ellen Grace O'Brian

LIVING THE ETERNAL WAY

SINGLE BLADE OF GRASS

ONE HEART OPENING

SANCTUARY OF BELONGING

Register to receive free daily email inspirations
by Rev. Ellen Grace O'Brian:

www.csecenter.org or email info@csecenter.org

Contents

Nothing separates us from God. It is only the acquired habit of identifying with modified mental states and objective phenomena that causes and sustains the illusion of independent existence. When this error in perception is corrected, our awareness is immediately restored to its original, pure wholeness.

—Roy Eugene Davis

Introduction
How to Live a God-Inspired Life
and Be Receptive to Your Good

One [supreme] Self is the ultimate Reality. It is the source of everything. The soul is immortal. God's attributes permeate it. Let your spiritual path be God-communion.

—Lahiri Mahasaya

When we live in the soul we live in the highest way, imbued with the radiance of God-communion. We live intentionally, following inner guidance rather than old habits or reactive patterns. This requires us to quiet our minds and open our hearts, release the past and live in the moment, free ourselves from doubt and worry and walk in the light of faith. In the following pages you will find inspiration and spiritual teachings to support your experience of 90 blessings in 90 days—insights into an enlightened way of living that reveals the blessedness of each day.

Some people think of enlightenment as an unattainable goal, or one realized by only a special few. But enlightenment is our natural state, the certain destiny of every person. When I met my spiritual teacher, Roy Eugene Davis, in 1979, he shared with me what his own teacher, Paramahansa Yogananda, had said to him: "Don't look back. Don't look to the left or to the right. Look straight ahead to the goal [of Self and God realization], and go all the way in this lifetime. You can do it." Let's turn our attention to life's highest potential for development and expect the best for ourselves and our world.

Begin your own 90 day program now, with chapters one through four and the daily inspirations that follow, drawing upon the radiance of your own divine Self to live a spiritually conscious life.

There is not in this world a kind of life more sweet and delightful than that of a continual walk with God. Those only can comprehend it who practice and experience it.

—Brother Lawrence
The Practice and Presence of God

Chapter One
Four Essentials for Spiritual Living

The fullness of joy is to behold God in everything.
—Julian of Norwich

The great Rabbi Abraham Joshua Heschel said, "Just to be is a blessing. Just to live is holy." His words ring like a call to prayer: wake up, be present, realize life is holy, experience the blessing of this moment; don't let this opportunity of a lifetime pass you by. This is the call to live a God-Inspired life, to awaken to our essential nature as conscious being, the one eternal Reality which is the source and substance of all that is. It is an invitation to realize through direct experience that we are not separate from God. Nothing separates us from God, nothing, ever—no condition, no belief, no past deed, no impure thought. We can never be separated from that which we are. We can think we are separate, we might feel as though we are, we might even believe that we are, but none of that can ever make it so. There is only one Life—God, the Single Reality expressing as all that is and ever will be. God is our life. Rabbi Heschel was right in saying "just to be is a blessing." We cannot be, cannot exist, without God, and with God, we are always blessed. Just to exist is to be of God. Knowing this truth liberates us from the burden created by the illusion of a separate self, restores us to wholeness and sets us free to experience life as the blessing it is. When life's holiness is revealed to us, living each day is an opportunity to discover what Paramahansa Yogananda called "ever-new joy in God. "

Until we know the spiritual truth about our essential nature it is difficult to "just be." Why? Because without realizing life's inherent wholeness, most people believe they have to work at life and struggle to win a competitive battle, if not for survival at least for security and happiness. But life is not meant to be a battle or a burden; we only make it so with our lack of awareness and our insistence on seeing ourselves as separate from God. If we imagine we are on our own, that God is some far off entity, or heavenly judge, we can be too busy trying to earn merit to discover the good that is already before us. Discovering life's goodness is not difficult, it just takes willingness and practice. When we embody our commitment to live a God-inspired life with congruent action we are met by divine grace, life's inherent support for awakening.

Four essential practices provide the foundation for the awakened life. They are: self inquiry; meditation and prayer; truthful living and embracing wholeness. Cultivating awareness through these four practices brings balance which contributes to inner peace and joy. Spiritual practice can and should be nourishing, ever leading to deeper insight, more skillful living, and the blossoming of the innate divine qualities of wisdom and compassion. No spiritual practice will ever make us spiritual, or improve upon our essential nature. The point of spiritual practice is to reveal the divine nature and qualities already with us, to allow the soul's radiance to shine through the mind and illumine the personality, transforming the once self-centered ego into an instrument for serving life. Deep within the heart of every person is a longing to belong, to love and be loved and to be of service, to make a contribution to life. This is the natural expression of our deepest desire to return to what we are.

Self inquiry is the practice of examining, through intention and focused attention, the nature of the self. Who, or what, are we? Even a little keen observation reveals that we are not essentially that which we can observe. We observe our thoughts, our feelings, and our bodies. Who or what is the observer? The practices of self inquiry and meditation naturally support one another as both require concentration to notice what arises and passes away and what remains. That we are what remains constant—the silent witness, that we are consciousness itself, is soon revealed.

Through meditation, we consciously move from the surface of life—from being aware primarily of sensory input and the contents of the thinking mind, to settling into the center of consciousness and experiencing ourselves as pure, essential being. This practice expands our awareness and makes it possible for us to see more clearly not only who we are, but the choices before us in any given moment regarding how we will respond to life. With meditation, we notice thoughts and feelings, and we notice that it is possible to be aware of them without reacting to them. We notice we can live in the soul; we can bring forth the light of awakened realization into all that we do. The peace of the soul pervades the mental field and the body during meditation, and then we consciously carry it forth into our day.

Truthful living is learning to do that which is in harmony with the highest good. It is not trying to be good; it is living in such a way that the divine qualities of our essential nature are revealed. The awakened heart naturally follows universal ethical precepts out of the realization of oneness. We see clearly that what we do to others we do to ourselves and we realize that our highest happiness is connected to the happiness of others.

Embracing wholeness is the practice of surrendering the sense of being separate from the one Source of all. It is accomplished through following both the avenues of discernment and devotion. Through discernment we recognize that the one life, power, and presence that nourishes and supports all of life is expressing as our own life. We see the One in all and relate to life as one reality appearing variously. The avenue of the heart supports us in experiencing that one reality as all-pervading Love, whose essential nature gracefully supports all forms of life in the fulfillment of their potential. We learn to surrender the sense of being separate by discovering how to harmonize our individual will with divine will. We learn how to cooperate with life's supportive influence and discover that we are radically supported. Taking the four practices of meditation, self inquiry, truthful living and embracing wholeness to heart and practicing them with sincere dedication transforms our lives.

Chapter Two
How to Be Sustained
by Daily Prayer and Meditation

Above all else, seek to know Reality and how to bring your will into harmony with It; the rest of what you need will be provided.

To illustrate the importance of meditation, Paramahansa Yogananda told the following story. A man received the great honor of being granted an appointment with the king. He arrived early at the palace, full of anticipation of the meeting. When he entered the palace grounds, he was awed by their beauty—cascading waterfalls, peacocks and other exotic birds, the sweet fragrance of flowers filling the air, fruit trees laden with delicious fruit, and beautiful music that permeated the atmosphere. As he wandered through the garden, around every turn he discovered a new delight. He was so entranced by his experience in the garden that he was unaware of the passing of time until the palace guard came to inform him that he had missed his opportunity to meet the king and he was escorted out of the garden. Paramahansaji would then offer the commentary that if the man had only kept his appointment with the king, he could have visited the palace grounds anytime.

This story is a parable of the soul's journey in the world. As spiritual beings, our "appointment with the king" is our opportunity to experience communion with God and through that meditative experience, realize the truth of what we are. Even though we are spiritual beings who have this divine appointment, we are often like the man in the story who becomes so distracted by his experience in the garden that forgets what he came for. This forgetful state of mind and distracted way of living is the condition of most people in our world today and it is the cause of much of the suffering in our world. All people are essentially pure Spirit expressing through a mind and body, journeying through this garden of earthly life but few know or remember the purpose for being here. Instead, they move through life on the surface of things, ignorant of the basic spiritual insight that reveals the causes and conditions that determine our life experience. Life is something that happens to them; they are the effect of conditions instead of conscious participants in their own destiny. They lack the awareness that there is another way to live, a way that brings the highest happiness. One who is spiritually awake has the ability to visit the garden, and enjoy it, anytime while remaining inwardly aware of his or her true purpose. Or, as Jesus taught, can live in the world but not be of it.

Meditation is focusing our awareness on our essential nature, or abiding in the Self. When we meditate, we arrange conditions so that we can experience that which is beyond our fleeting thoughts and emotions—the unchanging Self. This can be accomplished through a simple technique of concentrating on a single focus of attention until restless thought activity subsides.

To meditate, begin by sitting upright in a comfortable position that will allow you to remain still for a period of time. Close your eyes; take a couple of fully conscious breaths and gently intend to relax. Bless this time of inward focus with a moment of prayer. Address God in whatever way you think of God, opening your heart and mind to divine communion. Be receptive and remember that you are praying and meditating in God, rather than to

God. Remember that God is the source of your life, the ever present single Reality. Intend for your meditation to be conscious contact with God, realization of your spiritual nature. Meditation as a spiritual practice is not passive relaxation; it is clear focusing of our attention for the express purpose of clarifying our awareness.

Once you have begun to turn within by establishing a firm but relaxed meditation posture, closing your eyes, and offering a moment of prayer, begin to notice your breath, the natural rhythm of inhalation and exhalation. Observe the breath entering your nostrils and how it feels when it strikes the back of your throat. Notice the cool temperature of the air and how it becomes warmer on exhalation. Don't try to change the breath, simply be aware of it. Then proceed with your meditation by bringing your attention and inner gaze up to the spiritual eye, the point between and slightly above the eyebrows. To strengthen your concentration, imagine that your breath now moves through this subtle energy center, the spiritual eye. With inhalation, feel as if the air moves through this point, and with exhalation imagine that it exits the body from this point as well.

After attending to the breath for awhile and keeping the inner gaze focused at the spiritual eye, you can introduce a mantra, or word phrase, into the mental field to further support your concentration. Choose a simple word, or phrase such as "Om, God" or "Peace" that has a soothing effect on the mental field and contributes to clarity. Using the mantra "Om, God" mentally listen to the word "Om" with inhalation, and with exhalation, listen to the word "God." With each breath, let the remembrance of the word contribute to keeping attention focused, deepening relaxation and becoming receptive to inner experience. When the mental field becomes calm and clear, let go of the meditation techniques and simply rest in the silence while remaining inwardly aware. Let your inner gaze remain at the spiritual eye and gently look within and listen within, becoming receptive to inner light and inner sound. If thought activity arises and intrudes on the experience of meditation, simply return to the use of the word phrase and focus awareness on the breath.

When you are ready to conclude your meditation, take a moment to consciously invite the peace of your soul to permeate your mind and body. Feel that you are bathed in the light of divine consciousness, that your mind and body are refreshed and perfectly in balance. Pray for the happiness and well being of others, and for the healing and blessing of our world. Intend to take the peace of meditation with you into your day.

Chapter Three
Be Transformed by Renewing Your Mind

As we think in our hearts, so are we.
—Proverbs 23:7

The Buddha is quoted as saying, "with our thoughts we make the world…think or act with an impure mind and suffering will follow you like your shadow but think and act with a pure mind and joy will be your constant companion." The mind can be a great enemy or a great friend. When the mind is clouded and restless and obscures awareness of our true nature, we may be driven by habits and emotions that do not serve our highest good and bring suffering in their wake. Sometimes people feel trapped by their own reactive patterns and despair to know how to change them. Learning to change our thoughts patterns and to purify the mental field itself makes all the difference.

Transforming the mind is achieved with two basic methods in cooperation with divine grace and right living. Both methods require an expansion of awareness, discernment of inner subtle realities, learning to focus attention and purposeful intention.

The first step in working with the mind is to consider the nature of the mind and consciousness itself. What is the relationship of mind to soul? Of body to mind? Of our thoughts to our experiences? The true Self, our soul nature, expresses through mind and body. The mind is an instrument used by the soul; the light of awareness shining in the mental field is the light of Supreme Consciousness of which each soul is an individual expression. Mind alone is not conscious but our spiritual nature is ever conscious, ever aware. This distinction is important for us to know because it means that we, as conscious spiritual beings, can observe, influence and change our minds. And this is where transformation begins.

We begin by taking the perspective of the conscious witness to our thoughts and emotions. We observe what thoughts prevail in the mental field and we determine whether or not those thoughts are useful. Do they contribute to peace and well being? Are they true? Anytime we discover that the mental field is restless with thoughts that are not useful, that are not based in truth and promote a negative influence in our life we can simply introduce another train of thought.

One of the most potent practices to transform our experience is to cultivate the opposite. First we notice and acknowledge what we are thinking and feeling, and then we introduce another possibility into the mental field. If the mind is overrun with resentment, cultivate thoughts of forgiveness. If anger and hatred fill your mind, bring forth a new quality of mindful attention through thoughts of loving kindness. Sometimes people worry that they will deny important feelings if they substitute other thoughts and feelings. This practice is not denial of thoughts or feelings, but becoming more conscious of them. We notice our predominating thoughts and feelings and may even inquire into what brought them about. Then, we consciously decide to bring forth a more positive perspective so that any decisions we make or actions we take will be done in the clearest way. Changing our thought patterns from resentment to forgiveness does not give us amnesia. We don't forget what happened, we become better equipped to deal with it, with a loving heart and a calm mind. The decision to live in the soul, to live consciously in the highest way, means that we do not allow circumstances in life to control our reaction. Instead, we learn to respond to life and we realize that we can consciously choose to bring more clarity, more love, and more peace to each situation.

Changing the environment of the mind is accomplished through the practice of superconscious meditation, through repeated experiences of abiding in the Self, beyond involvement with thought activity, during the meditation experience. These occasions of spiritual clarity actually transform the mind itself. The mental field is purified and the experience of spiritual knowledge illumines the mind. Thoughts that are not consistent with spiritual truth do not long prevail in a mind that is filled with the light of the soul. Direct perception of our essential nature as Supreme Consciousness through higher states of meditation dispels confusion and heaviness from the mind. The peace of the soul prevails and its innate wisdom becomes more easily perceived through the purified mind. Inner guidance is more readily available. This is the key to living in the soul —regular immersion in superconsciousness, inviting the light of the soul to shine freely in the mind and opening to divine guidance from within to light up the path of right action. Then we have only to cooperate with what is revealed as the highest good ; we have only to live it. When we do, peace is our witness and the soul's joy our compass.

Perform all your duties with your hands;
let your heart be with God.

—Kabir

Chapter Four
90 Blessings, A Daily Spiritual Journal

*The joyous, spiritually conscious life rests upon simple choices—
choices made in ordinary moments each day.*

Embarking on the journey to experience 90 blessings in 90 days is simply a decision to live a spiritually conscious life, to make Self and God–realization the central focus of each day. Even if we fall into forgetfulness many times a day, the commitment to be spiritually awake and to turn to God as the polestar of our life contains within it God's graceful power that will support us in every way. In a difficult moment we may forget that we decided to look for the good and to live in the highest way, but the inherent goodness and supportive influence of God's grace will direct our attention toward the lighted the path before us. In that moment we will see the choice before us and it will be up to us.

The inspirations and affirmations that follow are for each day in the 90 day program. After your morning prayer and meditation, reflect on the thought of the day and as you are inspired, cultivate the affirmative thought or write your own affirmation to practice for that day. Know that you are guided by the inner light of God and that you will be met by divine grace in all that you do. Let your mind return to the affirmation during the day. Be open to opportunities to practice and notice what happens. Look for the good that comes your way and inwardly give thanks to God for all occasions of divine remembrance. What is it that turns the mind toward the light but the presence of Divine Light Itself? Realize that even the interest in spiritual practice is an indication that God's grace is already at work in your life.

At the end of each day, return to the inspiration and before retiring for the evening write one blessing, one moment of grace, or one moment of gratitude you were aware of that day in the open space on the page. If you cannot recall a single instant of divine remembrance or blessing then count the one you are presently in and write that down. Give thanks for the moment of reflection itself. It is only by bringing forth appreciation and blessing that blessings grow in our life—the eternal spiritual law of sowing and reaping at work.

Take the first step by making the commitment that for the next 90 days you will follow this simple spiritual path with its four essential practices: daily prayer and meditation, self-inquiry, truthful living and embracing wholeness. The daily inspirations are provided as stepping stones so that one day at a time the way of living in the soul is realized.

Welcome to the threshold of possibility.

Day One

Any spiritual discipline we practice is for our own sake, not for God. Our practice does not change God; it changes us. Spiritual practice helps us remove doubt, and experience directly the unconditional divine love that is already present within us.

I accept unconditional divine love now and open my consciousness to receive it. I engage in spiritual practice today because I do what is consistent with being aware, with loving and being loved. I know and affirm that I am love itself.

Day Two

The road to joy is paved with surrender.

I release the tendency to struggle with life and make it a burden. I open myself to joy as I let go of the illusion that I am on my own and remember that God is my ever present support.

Day Three

Two words must be relinquished to know peace: "if only."

I accept myself, others, and conditions in my life just as they are right now. I realize that the positive changes I can and will make today will arise from my inner peace.

Day Four

The divine name is a thread connected to the tapestry of God's ever-presence.

I practice the presence of God by remembering the divine name. Instead of letting my mind wander into worry or fear, I will inwardly call upon God and cultivate inner peace.

Day Five

Everything in this world is a fast moving current of change; only God remains changeless. Rely on God alone for support in every situation.

Today I will look through circumstances by remembering that everything changes and remind myself that God alone is my source of support.

Day Six

Live simply by recognizing what is most important each day.

Beginning this day with meditation and prayer, I take the time to nurture my spiritual awareness and to reflect on my priorities for today.

Day Seven

Set yourself free by setting others free.

I cleanse my heart and mind from any error thoughts of re-sentment or indebtedness. I realize that as long as I hold others in judgment, I am not free. I release the past; it has no power over me.

Day Eight

Love is already present in every situation today. Expect to meet love wherever you go.

I recognize the divine Self in everyone I meet. I bring the awareness of divine love with me wherever I go and realize that the One life is meeting Itself.

Day Nine

Draw a circle of unbroken awareness from your meditation cushion to every action in your day. The mind, dwelling in the conscious awareness of the presence of God, draws the circle.

My meditation continues in activity as I continually turn my mind to thoughts of God.

Day Ten

Like a great tree that drinks in the sun's rays at dawn and turns them in to shade for the weary passerby at noon, each morning drink from the fountain of God's love and become refreshment for those you meet.

To be a blessing will be my intention for today, by simply remembering that we are all of God. Quietly, inwardly, remembering this truth when I meet others blesses us both.

Day Eleven

We attain what the heart is fixed upon.

I will take the time today to reflect on what makes my heart sing with joy and fix my heart upon the highest good.

Day Twelve

Buddhi, or the discerning aspect of mind, is like an impartial judge who weighs inputs from the sensory cast of characters. Ego receives input from buddhi and decides which course of action is most beneficial to the self. A surrendered or purified ego will choose the course of action in harmony with the soul.

Before making important decisions today, I will ask: what will it serve? I will choose what serves my spiritual awakening and what is in harmony with divine will.

Day Thirteen

Balance renders life fruitful.

I use a gentle approach to bring my life into balance in those areas that need it. I know that a simple, single step toward my goal makes a difference.

Day Fourteen

We are capable of doing many things at once, such as driving our car while having a conversation with our friend who is a passenger. We can listen to our friend and respond, all the while keeping our attention on the road with awareness of our destination guiding our turns. In this same way, it is possible to work in the world and fulfill our responsibilities while inwardly engaging in prayer.

It will be my goal today to pray during activity. I will use windows of opportunity as moments of remembrance and turn my heart and mind to God.

Day Fifteen

Prayer of the heart is a prayer that arises spontaneously from divine love. When we are in love, there is no effort required to think of our beloved; our mind is captured by the heart.

Today I will allow myself the time to appreciate my life, to notice the beauty of nature and to open my mind to the blessing of being who I am.

Day Sixteen

Let your meditation be an effortless receiving of truth.
Simply sit still in the grace-bestowing presence.

*I realize that God is omnipresent and know that I meditate in
God's ever-presence. Nothing separates me from God.*

Day Seventeen

Life is ready and willing to give us all that we need in this moment. When we let go of the past, this truth is abundantly revealed.

God does not withhold. Everything that is for my good is already released. I let go of limiting beliefs and open my mind to infinite good.

Day Eighteen

Whenever something is taken away, look for the hand of love.

I turn my mind to the great purpose of my life: awakening. Today I will consider how all that occurs can be supportive of my spiritual awakening.

Day Nineteen

Renunciation does not require renouncing the world or
our duties in it. The abode of the true renunciate is the
cave of the heart. Everything done with nonattachment
and love for God in our hearts is renunciation.

*I will envision, set goals and work toward them while letting
go of my attachment to particular outcomes and knowing
that God brings forth the highest good according to divine
will. My overarching goal will be to do what I do with love.*

Day Twenty

Be suspicious of the thought that encourages you to begin to practice meditation tomorrow, or next week when you have finished some important work, or when more time is available. Everything depends on God. Begin today.

I realize that this life is not my own; it is God's life, and to live in harmony with God's will is the secret to my happiness and freedom. I take time to meditate today.

Day Twenty One

How can one accomplish single-minded devotion to God
in the midst of work and family life? See God in all. Serve
God in all. Do everything for God.

*I see and serve God in all I meet; everywhere I meet the one
divine Self in Its many forms.*

Day Twenty Two

Choose the way of life that leads to increased awareness, enhanced life, and love. Our own aliveness, the soul's deep abiding joy, can point the way.

I remain mindful of inner joy and choose what nurtures the soul.

Day Twenty Three

Search out the wily ways of self-interest. Sometimes it's in the driver's seat as we move toward a goal. Other times it encourages us to pull back and refuse to embrace our divine destiny with love and zeal.

I choose to live life beyond the boundaries of self interest. I celebrate my divine connection to all of life and I accept that true prosperity for me includes the well being of all.

Day Twenty Four

Above all, be steadfast in meditation. It is the boat that carries you across the river of delusion and keeps you from being lost in the whirlpools of anxious thought.

I treasure the time I set aside for meditation and chart my course to live an inspired life through daily divine communion.

Day Twenty Five

Meditation is not difficult. Getting beyond the ego's resistance to meditation—that can be difficult. For this, nothing but commitment realized through daily practice will suffice.

Daily meditation is a commitment I make to myself, a commitment to realize my greatest potential.

Day Twenty Six

Free yourself from faultfinding and faith will blossom.

I look for the good in all that I see and cultivate appreciation for life. I remember that divine order pervades all that is.

Day Twenty Seven

Don't think about changing the world or even how to serve the world. Think about changing yourself and how you can serve one person. Then serve with love.

I will look for the opportunities that arise today to be of service to another person and respond with love.

Day Twenty Eight

Spiritual knowledge amassed from books is like building a house of cards; a little troublesome wind will overturn it. But knowledge gained through direct perception is eternal, unshakable. Seek God in the "book" of your heart through daily, divine meditation.

I turn to God in the quiet sanctuary of my heart and bring a clear intention to meditation—to know God and to realize my own divine nature.

Day Twenty Nine

Once our innate divinity is revealed, we must act in accordance with it. True revelation purifies heart and mind, and spontaneous goodness—kindness in thought, speech, and action—springs forth like grasses after the rain.

I will be quick to follow those inspirations for simple acts of kindness that arise in my mind today.

Day Thirty

The key to freedom, security, and happiness is forged
from the practice of letting go of self-will. Without that
key, much of our energy is spent trying to get what we
want, or avoid what we don't want. Imagine being free of
all that. You are the locksmith.

*To let go of the limitations of self will I pause before I act and
open myself through prayer and willingness to follow divine
will.*

Day Thirty One

The feeling of being overwhelmed, experiencing life as a burden with too much to do, is often not caused by work. At the root of this difficulty is a break from living in harmony with our deepest values. When we live in accordance with our soul's wisdom, we are inwardly sustained.

I am in touch with what has heart and meaning for me and live in harmony with my deepest values.

Day Thirty Two

Ego is a seamstress who sews thoughts together to make the curtain that separates us from seeing the unity of life.

When thoughts that breed disharmony or separation arise I will greet them by silently saying "not two" as I recognize that the reality of God is one.

Day Thirty Three

The mind can conceive unity as an idea, but only as the opposite of separateness. The mind can never really know unity—that is the domain of the heart.

I honor the ability of my mind to discern differences and I remember that the experience of oneness transcends mind. I practice letting my mind sink into my heart, and realize the completeness that only stillness reveals.

Day Thirty Four

We find our greatest happiness in the open field of possibility, yet search endlessly for the shelter of certainty.

Today I'll remember that I do not have to know everything. I will enjoy life knowing that I can trust the divine plan that is unfolding.

Day Thirty Five

To be steadfast on your spiritual path, be attentive to your soul's joy. Let joy, the soul's delight, be your compass.

Since joy is natural to my soul I will attend to its presence and recognize it as an indicator of my spiritual well being.

Day Thirty Six

As we recognize the oak when we see the acorn, let us also recognize the potentials of our thoughts.

I cultivate those thoughts that are in alignment with my highest goals.

Day Thirty Seven

We cannot escape wholeness, yet we can fail to recognize it. Spiritual awakening is the realization of wholeness, beholding the One in all.

I am Spirit, expressing through my mind and body. I am free from the limiting perspective of identifying with the roles I play in life.

Day Thirty Eight

One who knows the truth is free from both pride and the delusion of inferiority. Self-esteem is the natural result of spiritual awakening. It is not a matter of degrees. We either know who we are or we do not.

I see everyone, including myself, through the eyes of love. We are all expressions of the one divine life, each one precious.

Day Thirty Nine

We live in a world of pure possibility. Open the window of your mind.

I embrace the mystery of life and open myself to ever new possibilities. There is an unseen power for good, greater than what can be known, and I can learn to cooperate with It.

Day Forty

Great souls know nothing of failure. At every turn, they see the opportunity to learn.

Holding the goal of awakening ever before me, even a mistake can be a blessing. With any mistake I have the opportunity to strengthen my character—this is of real value.

Day Forty One

As life unfolds from within, it is natural for our vision to be ahead of physical manifestation. The space between the two is connected by faith.

Outer appearances are the effect of my vision, not the cause. My vision is already realized in consciousness; I accept the truth of my experience as I walk in faith remaining open to the unfolding of the vision.

Day Forty Two

Criticism can be seductive when it masquerades as an attempt to help. Consider the energy it takes to criticize and the effect it has on the spirit of both parties. Real help lifts the spirits of everyone involved.

Today I will offer a kind word, an encouraging word, an affirmative word and notice the effect it has on me.

Day Forty Three

Choose high ideals that are worthy of you and let them guide your life. Without high ideals, we can too easily become involved with things that do not matter. Chart your course.

My actions rest on my consciously chosen core values. I remain focused on what truly matters to me and live with purpose.

Day Forty Four

Do not strive to fix the world; that is arrogance. Instead, love the world as your own self and strive to change any part of your life that does not speak this truth.

Love is not just a word from my mouth but my commitment to living in the highest way. I am willing to grow, to change, and to become an instrument of peace.

Day Forty Five

Peace comes in a moment but takes a lifetime to realize. It is not something we attain; it is a way of life. Fill your day with peaceful moments that become a peaceful life.

I will use the windows of opportunity that open to me to cultivate peace by simply bringing full awareness to my breath and inviting the soul's peace to fill my mind and body.

Day Forty Six

Trusting God is the willingness to actively wait for clarity. Faith holds the time of not knowing as a fisherman holds his line.

I trust that greater good than I can even imagine is moving through my life and arranging conditions for the highest good. I remain open to the truth and higher understanding that will be revealed to me.

Day Forty Seven

Prayer aligns our body, mind, and spirit. With prayer, we can keep our balance. Without it, one part of our nature is compromised and another over-developed. Prayer is the key to harmony with self and others.

I will make prayer my priority—start my day with prayer, pause throughout the day for a moment of prayer and end the day with prayer.

Day Forty Eight

Humility is bending to God's will. It is fulfilled through the absolute willingness to be who we are as expressions of God.

I have the courage to be completely who I am, to speak and live the truth and to trust that I am divinely supported as God's own beloved.

Day Forty Nine

Live simply. Ask: what is the one useful thing I can do to-day that I know is in harmony with divine will? Do that.

Today I will do the one thing that calls to me, that one thing which I know is essential.

Day Fifty

Turning to God with the expectation that it will improve a human condition signifies a conflicted mind, straddling the viewpoints of duality and wholeness. Turn to God and accept healing now.

I let go of clinging to the past, and open myself to accept the healing that is now.

Day Fifty One

Worry stirs up the mind and blocks our access to inner peace and, ultimately, right action. When worry arises, acknowledge the concern and then bring forth the self-care that will restore balance and inner peace.

If worry surfaces in my mind I will use it as a reminder to engage in self care and regain my balance. Then I will consider all in the light of inner peace.

Day Fifty Two

Gratitude is an antidote to worry. We can adjust our mental and spiritual condition through appreciation and praise. Let your inner light shine by acknowledging what is good.

I will sweep my mind of worry with the cleansing power of gratitude. I will bring forth appreciation and praise for the goodness that surrounds me.

Day Fifty Three

Gratitude is not a feeling; it is an attitude. We can practice it regardless of how we feel in any given moment. When we cultivate an attitude of gratitude regardless of external conditions, we magnetize our awareness for good and contribute to peace.

In every situation the potential for experiencing gratitude exists. I will search it out and call it forth.

Day Fifty Four

Live in the world as a spiritual being. Rely on the infinite resourcefulness of Divine Consciousness by knowing that the activity of Truth in your own mind and consciousness will provide the necessary direction.

I open myself to divine wisdom and seek inner guidance knowing that as the potentials of God exist within me, I am infinitely resourceful.

Day Fifty Five

Your heart is the altar, the center of consciousness where God dwells. Make a pilgrimage there today.

The journey to the heart takes only a moment—a moment of practicing the presence of God as the indwelling presence in the temple of the heart.

Day Fifty Six

Our journey of spiritual awakening begins the moment we accept responsibility for our life experience.

I free myself from any temptation to live as a victim as I realize that my life experience is powerfully molded by my choices, and I choose to be aware.

Day Fifty Seven

Both good and bad habits are the children of our thought process. We bring them into being and support them with attention. Then we become convinced they are a part of us we cannot do without. We can change any habit once we see clearly how we created it.

I affirm the power within me that is greater than the hold of any habit. Just as I have put old habits in place by choosing them again and again, today I make a new choice.

Day Fifty Eight

If we want to live in peace and in joy we must be committed to it. This requires vigilant attention to our state of mind and the willingness to use our soul-inspired wisdom to redirect our thoughts from negativity to thoughts that are uplifting.

Today I will bring special attention to my thoughts and choose those that are consistent with my commitment to experience inner peace and the soul's joy.

Day Fifty Nine

Guidance for healthy living shines continuously from the wisdom of the soul, yet sense attachments, self-will, and habit, may overshadow it. Seek the soul's wisdom before taking action.

A simple pause, a moment of inner reflection, before taking important actions will be my practice today.

Day Sixty

Believe in your Self. Know that it is possible for you to experience the reality of God because God is your life. Let this faithful confidence inspire your daily spiritual practice.

I approach my spiritual practice with the clear intention to realize Truth. Self realization is my certain destiny.

Day Sixty One

Attachment to the results of our actions binds us to time.
Work with integrity in the present moment and let the
future unfold in divine order.

*When my mind moves into thinking about the future, I will
consciously return to what is right in front of me and give my
full attention to what I am doing in the moment.*

Day Sixty Two

When the soul returns to abide in Spirit, consciousness moves from dwelling in the individual apartment of the body-mind to the omnipresent expanse of infinite joy, creative possibility, and pure knowledge. This is possible anytime.

I abide in Spirit, my true nature.

Day Sixty Three

When we live with faith in a vision, we are inspired toward actions that support that vision. We become aware of the opportunities that present themselves that otherwise may go unnoticed.

I notice an abundance of opportunities each day and I use my discernment to determine if they are in alignment with my vision.

Day Sixty Four

Each day the door to spiritual fulfillment opens to us. Life continually presents us with opportunities to be awake, to love, and to serve.

A simple goal: today I will learn something. I will demonstrate my love for someone and I will be of service.

Day Sixty Five

The prayer to be God's instrument is not a passive prayer. It requires our willingness to speak the word, sing the song, mend the relationship, and do the work that is inspired.

I take a step toward my vision of fulfillment today, doing what needs to be done to follow my inspiration.

Day Sixty Six

Imagine what it would be like to accept life as it is and to accept yourself just as you are. Let go of the conversation in your mind about things needing to be different than they are and watch what happens. When there is no desire for life to be different than it is, peace arrives.

In this moment I accept myself, others, and circumstances just as they are. With this acceptance I open myself to seeing more clearly.

Day Sixty Seven

To walk with God on the path of life is to put God first, to do what we do and remember God. When we have faith in God, we remember that God is our Life, the Source of all good, happiness, and security.

I will seek God out in the activity of my day through remembering that my life is God's life and I am completely supported in the highest way.

Day Sixty Eight

When we allow something other than God to fully occupy our minds, when we put it first in our thoughts and our concerns, we put another "god" before God. We give it power and it starts to rule our life.

I will free myself from the tyranny of false gods, concerns that seem to loom large, by holding to what is true—knowing that God can and will meet every need.

Day Sixty Nine

If we are always focused on getting somewhere, we never arrive. Be here now and notice the wonder, the beauty, the grace, and the love that is present.

I will savor life today, taking the time to breathe in the richness of the present moment.

Day Seventy

The spiritual practice of cultivating fearlessness is the willingness to trust God completely. Right where we are, in whatever situation we are in, the resources that are necessary to transform ourselves and our lives are within us. Be not conformed to this world, but be transformed by the renewing of your mind.

Love, not fear, guides me. I know that the Lord of Love dwells within me and guides my every step. I trust my inner guidance.

Day Seventy One

Every good thing that is intended for you according to God's grace will come to you; nothing can prevent it. Knowing this can transform your life.

I release my self from the fear of somehow missing out on life's goodness. The good that God has planned for me is already mine; I am receptive to it.

Day Seventy Two

What makes your heart sing with joy? Consider that at all times.

Today I will attend to my inner, felt, experience of life and be especially aware of joy when it arises.

Day Seventy Three

Attachment to particular outcomes can prevent us from fulfilling our potential.

I am open to the divine plan for my life that supports the fulfillment of my highest potential. I know that plan is likely greater than any outcome I have imagined.

Day Seventy Four

In the way of divine love, the mind turns toward God. Like a flower seeks the sun and opens in beauty before it, so the divine qualities of our true nature blossom forth through devotion.

Thoughts of God, the Highest Good, fill my mind and I express the divine potentials within me.

Day Seventy Five

Be active in the world but see to it that God occupies the throne of your heart and the court of your mind.

As I work in the world I cultivate divine remembrance. My heart and mind are purified with the light of surrendered devotion to God.

Day Seventy Six

Choose a lifestyle that is consistent with your life goal. A conscious spiritual life is not possible without self-discipline, just as climbing a mountain is not possible without a commitment to the goal and persistent action in support of it.

I erase the erroneous line between my spiritual and physical life by living according to my spiritual values and making wise choices that reflect my heart's desire.

Day Seventy Seven

The spiritual life is the way of effortless effort, striving without attachment to results. Do the work at hand with full concentration while your heart remains absorbed in divine remembrance.

As I release the burden that attachment to results brings I open my self to freedom and to the experience of effort-less effort.

Day Seventy Eight

When there is desire for the fruit of action, the mind travels between the present moment and the imagined future. By trying to grasp future good fortune we stir up a dust storm in the mind and lose touch with the joy of the present moment.

Nothing can come in the future that is not already present in potential. I will seek out that which I hope for in the temple of the present.

Day Seventy Nine

The Divine Self is omnipresent, no less present within each one of us. Learn to redirect the urge to look outside of yourself for solutions to problems. Look first to the potential within. Then be receptive to the resources that flow into your life through the power of your consciousness.

I will quiet the noise of my mind through meditation and patiently await insight and inspiration knowing that I can draw from the well of inner resources.

Day Eighty

When we are on friendly terms with our Self, we see goodness all around us. When we are at odds with our Self, being in the world is a constant struggle.

I will imagine that the world is my mirror and look for ways to polish that mirror by purifying my heart.

Day Eighty One

A person who has mastered himself or herself will have no problem with others. A sure sign of self-mastery is the ability to perceive others with an equal eye, recognizing God in all, the one Self playing all the roles.

Everywhere I look I see the one divine life of God. I celebrate the richness of God's cast of characters in this divine drama while remembering that everyone is greater than the role they play.

Day Eighty Two

Who is our friend? Who is our enemy? Most people have experienced that even the same person can play both roles. Who hasn't had a lover or a friend betray her trust? When this happens the good, admirable, likable qualities of that person seem to vanish overnight. Was this person the reason for our joy? Are they now the reason for our sorrow? Realize the true source of joy and be free.

I will search out the unconditional joy that arises from within and free myself from being tossed about by the wind of changing circumstances.

Day Eighty Three

God directs our steps as we rely upon God one step
at a time.

*I can take the step I see without having to know what the
next one will be; I trust it will be revealed in divine ways.*

Day Eighty Four

Acceptance is the simple way to contentment. We open the door to true happiness when we stop trying to make others, circumstances, or the world conform to our desires.

I will cultivate contentment in all circumstances and open the door to allow true happiness to enter.

Day Eighty Five

We are Supreme Consciousness Itself. We look for well-being, but we are well-being. We search for wholeness, but we are wholeness. We desire prosperity and security. We already are that. We pray for love. We are love itself.

Today I will stop searching and consider that life is one, seamless and whole.

Day Eighty Six

Only ego tries to get rid of ego. Don't fall into the spiritual trap of working on yourself to become spiritual. Be aware. Live in love, live in peace, and live in joy. That is all.

At the core of my being—spiritual perfection! Conscious living reveals that.

Day Eighty Seven

When we experience that we are whole, nothing external is needed for fulfillment. This leaves us free to participate as we are divinely guided and to appreciate the beauty of things in life without always having to possess them.

I find freedom in generosity, and I enter the stream of life's abundance as I share it.

Day Eighty Eight

Controversy keeps everyone busy except the lover of God.

Thoughts and opinions change but God, the Eternal Self, remains constant. In God's constancy and generosity, there is room for diversity.

Day Eighty Nine

Depending on the inspiration of others is like drinking thin soup— it doesn't satisfy strong hunger. Draw from the well of divine communion and cook up the nourishing soup of your own inner knowing.

I will drink from the well of divine communion today and be nourished by my own experience of the spiritual life.

Day Ninety

We develop into that which occupies our consciousness. So a devotee of God shines with the divine qualities of wisdom, compassion, patience and joy regardless of outer training or circumstances. The great reservoir of the soul's beatitude overflows into the personality. When we are established in the true Self, a channel has opened.

I turn to God, my higher true Self, reflect on the qualities of God, and encourage the divine potentials within me to be expressed.

Self-realization can definitely be accomplished by every reasonably intelligent person who chooses to live a well-ordered life and to nurture their spiritual growth. Their awakening will then progress from ordinary, egocentric states of consciousness to superconsciousness, cosmic consciousness, Self-realization, and God-realization. The culmination of right endeavor is complete, permanent liberation of consciousness.

The side benefits of spiritual practice—improved physical health, peace of mind, harmonious relationships, comfortable circumstances, and the ability to live more effectively—can be appreciated. It should be remembered, however, that the ultimate purpose for spiritual practice is to be Self-realized.

—Roy Eugene Davis
From *Paramahansa Yogananda as I Knew Him*

Center for Spiritual Enlightenment

Our message at CSE emphasizes the certain destiny for all people to awaken, and the importance of living a spiritually conscious life by following the universal precepts of the world's wisdom traditions such as harmlessness, truthfulness, and right use of life energy. We are all here to awaken to the truth that this life is God's life. We come from a common Source, live and move and have our being in that Source, and return to It. Awakening to the unity of life brings new joy in living and a clear sense of how we can each contribute to the well being of all.

We are dedicated to spiritual awakening by fostering an oasis of peace in the community, the world, and in the hearts of individuals.

For a schedule of programs or to contact Rev. Ellen Grace O'Brian:

Center for Spiritual Enlightenment
1146 University Avenue San Jose, CA 96126
(408) 283-0221
www.csecenter.org
email info@csecenter.org

Awaken to the One Truth known by many names